# GIVE ME A SIGN!

## What Pictograms Tell Us Without Words

### by Tiphaine Samoyault

**VIKING**

VIKING
Published by the Penguin Group
Penguin Books USA Inc., 375 Hudson Street, New York, New York 10014, U.S.A.
Penguin Books Ltd, 27 Wrights Lane, London W8 5TZ, England
Penguin Books Australia Ltd, Ringwood, Victoria, Australia
Penguin Books Canada Ltd, 10 Alcorn Avenue, Toronto, Ontario, Canada M4V 3B2
Penguin Books (N.Z.) Ltd, 182–190 Wairau Road, Auckland 10, New Zealand

Penguin Books Ltd, Registered Offices: Harmondsworth, Middlesex, England

First published in 1995 in France under the title *Le Monde des Pictogrammes* by Circonflexe
This English translation first published in 1997 in the United States of America by Viking,
a division of Penguin Books USA Inc.

1  3  5  7  9  10.  8  6  4  2

Copyright © Circonflexe, 1995
Translation copyright © Penguin Books USA Inc., 1997
All rights reserved
Translated by Esther Allen
Icon Illustrations by Fabienne Auguin
Design by Frederique Faudot

LIBRARY OF CONGRESS CATALOGING-IN-PUBLICATION DATA
Samoyault, Tiphaine.
[Monde des pictogrammes. English]
Give me a sign! : what pictograms tell us without words / by Tiphaine Samoyault.    p.    cm.
ISBN 0-670-87466-3
1. Signs and symbols—Juvenile literature.  2. Picture-writing—Juvenile literature.
3. Visual communication—Juvenile literature.  I. Title.
P53.7.S2613  1997  302.23—dc21    96-51985  CIP  AC

Printed in France
Set in Gill Sans

# Communicating with the World

In a car or on a train, in airports or train stations, at the movies or in school, at home or in a different country, everywhere you go you see small drawings that give you instructions (like don't smoke or no left turn), or tell you where to find an emergency exit, a restaurant, a gas station . . .

**These wordless signs are called pictograms.**

Pictograms were invented to make simple communication easier for people who speak different languages. They use drawings or symbols that can be understood by people from all over the world.

Ever since international travel became popular and international organizations such as the United Nations were formed, there has been more need for signs that can be understood by speakers of many different languages. Although many modern signs appeared only at the end of the last century, signs also existed—less formally— in civilizations of the past. What's new about modern signs is that, using pictograms, they form their own useful, coherent language—a language of pictures.

Since it first appeared, however, this new international language has gone through many changes.

## How? Why?

**That's what you'll learn on this journey through signs in history and around the world.**

# What Does "Pictogram" Mean?

The word **pictogram** has two roots: the Latin **"pictus,"** which means "painted," and the Greek **"gramma,"** which means "writing."

**"Pictogram" means a painted or drawn image that is used to stand for a written word or phrase.**

"Pictogram" was formed on the pattern of an older word, "ideogram," which means a drawing that represents an idea (either the object pictured or an idea associated with it). A pictogram is a kind of ideogram. A pictogram symbolizes a particular thing, but not a specific word for it. So a picture of a telephone can communicate the same thing to people from many different countries, even though they would each use a different word for it.

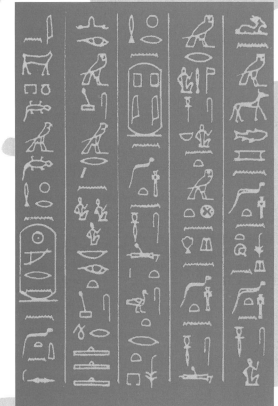

*Egyptian hieroglyphs.*

Some of the hieroglyphs that were used in ancient Egypt were pictograms, but not all of them. Hieroglyphs sometimes represent real objects, as most pictograms do (for example, the hieroglyph that means "lion" looks like a lion), or they may refer to an idea, as many ideograms do, or they may just represent a specific sound.

*Ideograms are used in Chinese writing.*

## THERE ARE THREE DIFFERENT KINDS OF PICTOGRAMS:

### Figurative Pictograms

These pictograms represent the object or action they refer to. The sign looks like the thing.

### Schematic Pictograms

The design of these pictograms is simplified and suggests what they represent schematically, that is, only by a very general outline. People understand these pictograms because they are used to seeing them.

*This square with an arrow in an opening on one side is one sign for an emergency exit, because an arrow usually indicates direction: the arrow symbolizes the movement of a person walking in a particular direction.*

*The Aztecs used a footprint to represent direction. This was a figurative pictogram.*

*Later a drawing of a hand was used. It was also a figurative pictogram.*

*Nowadays, instead of a drawing of any particular object, an arrow is used; it's more schematic but everyone can understand it.*

In this type of pictogram, the image must remain recognizable enough to make clear the relationship between the sign and what it suggests.

### Abstract Pictograms

These pictograms don't represent any specific object. They form a code that can only be understood by people who have learned it. In many countries, road signs are abstract pictograms. A bar is often used to mean something is forbidden, so this sign on a street corner means "do not enter."

# A Little History

**Before writing existed, people used pictograms without knowing it. When they wanted to communicate, they drew what they saw. But many thoughts were too abstract or complicated to put into pictures. People needed a more abstract system that would let them express all of their thoughts in written form. That's why alphabets were invented.**

Although an alphabet could express more than pictograms, it was a less universal form of writing, since it could only communicate ideas in a specific language. About a century ago people began realizing how useful it would be if signs with important simple messages could be written so that speakers of different languages anywhere in the world could understand. So they began to use pictograms in a new way. Road signs were the first modern pictograms.

The development of automobiles brought increased traffic and traffic accidents, so a system of road signs that everyone could understand was needed.

In 1895, the Italian Touring Club created the first road signs, and in 1909, the first international road signs were put in place.

Some of those signs have changed since then, in the same way that cars and clothes have changed over the

*The signs shown above warn drivers that an intersection is ahead, that left turns are forbidden, that they are approaching a hidden or dangerous bend, or that the road is slippery when wet.*

years. Others are still the same today.

After the first World War, tourism and international travel became much more common. Many researchers worked to invent a system that would ease the language barrier, creating new signs that anyone could understand.

In the 1930s, Otto Neurath, an Austrian philosopher, became interested in the language of images and created many pictograms. But it was not until the elegant pictograms created by the Japanese designer Katzumie Masaru for the Olympic Games held in Tokyo in 1964 that the idea of international pictograms really began to catch on.

An international event like the Olympic Games shows how much pictograms are needed; thanks to pictograms, athletes and visitors from across the world can easily find their way to the different places where competitions are held and can recognize the various types of events.

Like road signs, the pictograms that illustrate the different kinds of sporting events have continued to evolve. We can see how much these pictograms have changed since 1948.

*The Olympic flag symbolizes the union of the five continents joined together by sports: each color corresponds to a different part of the world.*

These pictograms, used at the Olympic Games held in London in 1948, show an *object* that is representative of each type of sporting event: for example, a pommel horse for gymnastics, boxing gloves, and a soccer ball.

The pictograms for the Tokyo Games in 1964 emphasized the *movements* of the athletes involved in the event.

For the Mexico City Games in 1968, the pictograms again showed the *equipment* used (next page).

At the Olympic Games in Munich in 1972, athletes and equipment were represented together in simplified forms and stylized poses (below).

The Los Angeles Games of 1984 showed a more detailed body and minimized the equipment; this has continued to be the trend (below).

In 1980, the Moscow Olympic Games returned to the idea of showing a symbolic gesture against a colored background (above right).

This type of variation can be found everywhere and in every situation, since each country selects images that reflect its own traditions.

## Different countries also use colors differently.

**Yellow** is very easy to see; that's why the Japanese use it as a background on signs that warn drivers about possible dangers.

In the West, **red** is considered an aggressive color: it is believed to attract a driver's attention. Stop signs and stop lights are both red, and European countries outline danger signs in red so that they will be noticed right away.

*In Europe, road signs that indicate danger are triangular and outlined by a red band; in Japan they are diamond shaped and bright yellow.*

The specific dangers, obstacles, or animals to watch out for are not necessarily the same everywhere. Here are some signs used by different countries to mark places where animals cross the road.

*In Australia, signs warn that a kangaroo or a koala may cross; in France, signs show a variety of animals, including deer, sheep, and cattle.*

**The same idea can be expressed by different pictures in different places at different times, but they always have the same goal: to give information in the clearest way possible.**

# Going on Vacation

## IN THE CAR

**Every car trip gives you a chance to see a lot of pictograms both inside the car and along the road.**

Sometimes pictograms are painted right on the road's surface. For instance, these arrows tell the driver which lanes may be used for making turns.

Some pictograms indicate how the car works. These are located on the dashboard. The ones below tell you about the lights on the car.

Sometimes they light up when something is wrong: then they are called warning lights.

The signs below give information about problems with the battery, fan, temperature, oil, gas, or brakes.

Others have to do with the security and comfort of the driver or passengers. They tell you to fasten your seatbelt and shut all doors.

## ON THE ROAD

**Road signs use pictograms that can be understood immediately by anyone who knows how the sign system works. They help to ensure that traffic will move safely and rapidly.**

Sometimes different colors are used as a way to indicate what category a sign belongs in.

*Red for signs forbidding drivers to do something.*

At the beginning of the century, every country adopted its own traffic regulations, but today the rules are defined by international agreement. Traffic signs are not the same in all countries, but they share some important features.

In Europe, the road signs used to indicate things that drivers are required to do or forbidden to do are round. This shape, which is rarely seen in an environment filled with vertical and horizontal lines—buildings, houses, and straight roads—immediately draws the driver's attention.

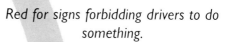

*Blue for signs providing important information.*

The two warning signs above are quite rare nowadays, since pushcarts and horse-drawn carriages are no longer seen very often! So you see, the signs we use also change as economic and technological developments change the kind of messages we need to communicate.

Different shapes of road signs are intended to alert the driver to something, too. You can find diamonds, octagons, triangles with the point up, and triangles with the point down.

Because these shapes are less common in the natural environment, they immediately attract the eye, especially the triangles, which work as visual commands.

The signs that indicate danger usually have an aggressive shape and a bright color.

Certain signs are intended to protect drivers from natural dangers such as falling rocks.

Other signs warn drivers to watch out for the other users of the road: children, bicyclists, animals, and so on.

## ALONG THE ROAD

**Pictograms are also used to indicate places where travelers can eat, fill up the gas tank, or rest for a while. These symbols usually appear on blue, white, or green backgrounds, which are nonaggressive colors that suggest relaxation.**

In parking lots or rest stops, other pictograms specify what is and is not allowed. For example, trash should not be thrown on the ground; it must be put in the garbage cans. Some water is not safe to drink.

At campgrounds, pictograms tell vacationers what areas should be used for tents or for campers, and where to find the restrooms.

*A sign from France suggests that tossing away a lit match might set fire to the surrounding forest.*

*Handicapped access.*

*Restrooms (called water closets in parts of Europe).*

Pictograms are used on vehicles transporting materials that are dan-

There are some signs you will find only at a ski resort or near a hiking trail.

gerous to the environment. These stickers warn other people about the product that is being transported. People will know they should be careful around trucks carrying flammable or hazardous substances.

# Traveling

**Travelers need to be able to find certain kinds of information even if they don't speak the language of the country.**

It's very difficult to create a symbol that people of all countries can recognize for men's and women's restrooms.

The figures of a woman in a skirt and a man in pants are a Western way of representing the distinction between the sexes; trying to represent this difference in any other way becomes complicated.

*The men's and ladies' rooms can be represented by well-known characters.*

Men and women do not wear skirts and pants in all countries. The solution might be to use the biological symbols for male and female, which are international. However, these signs are completely abstract, so they can only be read by people who know the code.

## IN A TRAIN STATION

In train stations, many of the services offered to travelers are marked by pictograms. Pictograms are also used in train stations to warn of dangers and indicate rules.

*Here, for example, travelers are told not to throw anything on the tracks and to place trash in the trash receptacles in the trains.*

*Places where baggage can be checked are also found in train stations. When you're on the train, the sign on the right warns you not to open or touch doors until it has stopped.*

## AT THE AIRPORT

Pictograms along the road tell you that an airport is nearby. They can take several different forms, but they will usually show some kind of airplane shape.

Airports are internationally important places that people from many different countries pass through. Passengers must be able to find their way around even if they do not know the language of the country they are in. Pictograms help them find what they need.

Airport signs are not standard, so sometimes you have to guess a little to figure them out.

*These drawings indicate the place where baggage can be checked or claimed and where tickets can be purchased.*

*The places where passengers go through customs may be marked in many ways.*

In other public places, pictograms indicate where the services that you may need can be found. The symbols vary a little from country to country but usually the signs will show a simple object such as a fork or a cup that can be easily recognized. Some signs, such as one indicating a pharmacy, use widely known traditional symbols. The message can usually be understood, thanks to the international codes.

These images designate the nearby presence of:

*A place to reserve a hotel room*

*A place to change money*

*A pharmacy*

*A post office*

*An information desk*

*A place to have a hot drink*

*A restaurant*

In France, the pictogram above indicates the presence of an information desk. The letter *i* indicates a place where you can find answers and information. But the word information does not begin with an *i* in all languages. So in many other countries, a question mark is used to designate a place where you can ask questions, instead.

*A taxi stand*

*A bus stop*

# IN PUBLIC PLACES

**The same pictograms can be used to show what you are allowed to do and what is prohibited.**

*Here, dogs are permitted.*

*Here, they are not.*

*Smoking is allowed here.*

*This is a no-smoking area.*

"Pull" or "Push" is sometimes written on doors, though a simple arrow is enough.

The pictogram representing an emergency exit has changed and

*Pull*

*Push*

been simplified over time. Nowadays, the international sign for an emergency exit is the picture shown

below; though it's a little schematic, it still looks like a person going out a door.

Stairs and escalators are often marked by big signs that are easy to see.

# Everyday Pictograms

Every day, ordinary activities are carried out with the help of pictograms. Even if you're not always aware of their presence, they provide you with a lot of handy information when you use the things around you.

The development of international markets means that the same products can be sold in many different countries. Since pictograms are more nearly universal than words, they can be found on products like refrigerators, sewing machines, and washing machines. The signs below give information about different kinds of refrigerators and how long they will preserve frozen foods.

*A symbol may appear on or near a doorbell.*

**Pictograms make it easier for people to use household products or appliances correctly.**

When you wash an article of clothing, the pictograms on the label indicate the temperature and cycle to

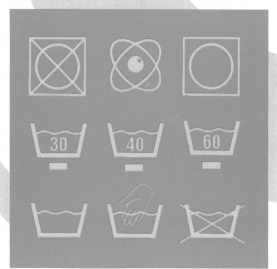

use when washing, or if something should be washed by hand.

*These signs tell whether something can be ironed.*

*The warning symbols for high-voltage electricity or radioactivity.*

## DANGEROUS PRODUCTS

Certain products are dangerous if they aren't handled with care:

*Poisonous product    Flammable product*

## MORTAL DANGER

Sometimes mortal danger is signaled by a skull. On the flags of pirate ships, the skull and crossbones warned that no one who encountered the ship would survive, so they came to symbolize death. Today, the skull warns us of danger from such things as electricity or hydraulic activity.

## FRAGILE, HANDLE WITH CARE!

When you receive a package, pictograms show how to treat it, especially if it should be handled with care:

*This should be held carefully or contains breakable objects.*

*This is recyclable or reusable.*

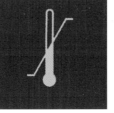 

*This can be damaged by high temperatures or humidity.*

# JOURNALISM

In some newspapers, pictograms enable readers to find the different sections quickly, without having to read through them.

Interviews

Movie reviews

## HOROSCOPES

These signs represent the twelve constellations of the zodiac, one of which is dominant when every person is born. The horoscope for the sign that corresponds to your birth date is supposed to tell your future. Here are the original symbols:

Cancer

Virgo

Leo

Gemini

Aquarius

Pisces

Aries

Taurus

Libra

Scorpio

Sagittarius

Capricorn

**Pictograms do more than just help people find their way around. They are an international system allowing people who speak many different languages to understand information right away. They are an important part of our modern global civilization.**

# Signs Throughout the World

Today, we can't imagine what it would be like to communicate only by simple drawings. Pictograms don't allow us to make sentences or to express abstract or complex thoughts. Their use remains limited, and travelers in foreign countries still end up having to ask for directions—at least some of the time.

However, pictograms are useful in a world that places a high value on efficiency and rapid communication. They remind us that all writing is an agreed-upon system of signs, and such systems are one thing that makes humankind unique.

# GLOSSARY

*abstract pictogram*: a pictogram that uses an image which does not show anything that is obviously related to the meaning of the sign. It is a symbol, but not a picture of anything.

*code*: a system of signals or symbols used to communicate. Knowledge of the way a code works (the *key*) is needed to understand it.

*figurative pictogram*: a pictogram that uses a picture of the object referred to, so that the sign looks like the thing.

*hieroglyphs*: pictures, usually representing words or sounds, that were used by priests to write down stories and messages in ancient Egypt. A hieroglyph is one particular sign. The system of signs is called *hieroglyphics*.

*ideogram*: a picture or symbol used to represent a thing or an idea but not a particular word or phrase for it.

*octagon*: an eight-sided figure, such as a stop sign.

*pictogram*: a painted or drawn image that is used to stand for a written word or phrase.

*schematic pictogram*: a pictogram that uses a very general design suggesting an object to represent an idea. It succeeds in communicating a message because it depicts something that people reading it are used to seeing and that they already understand.

*symbol*: something, especially a picture or a mark, that stands for something else.

1998